Where
Are
Those
Miracles?

Releasing The Power Of God

I John 4:16,17

Bishop Van I. Sharpe

Bishop Van I. Sharpe

Where Are Those Miracles?

Releasing The Power Of God

PENDIUM
PUBLISHING HOUSE
514-201 DANIELS STREET
RALEIGH, NC 27605

For information, please visit our Web site at
www.pendiumpublishing.com

PENDIUM Publishing and its logo
are registered trademarks.

Where Are Those Miracles?
Releasing The Power Of God
By Bishop Van I. Sharpe

ISBN: 978-1-944348-42-7

Unless otherwise indicated, Bible quotations are taken from The Authorized King James
Version, Copyright 2000 by The Zondervan Corporation, and The Amplified Bible,
Copyright 1954, 1958, 1964, 1965, 1987 by The Lockman Foundation, and The Message:
The Bible in Contemporary Language, Copyright 2002 by Eugene H. Peterson, and The
Living Bible, Copyright 1971 by Tyndale House Publishers, Wheaton, Illinois, and The
New International Version of the Bible, Copyright 1973, 1978, 1984 by International
Bible Society.

Front cover photograph by Solomon's Photography in Winterville, N.C.
Back cover photograph of the author by Terry Johnson
P. O. Box 1411
Tarboro, N.C. 27886
Tel. 252-469-5188 E-mail: tireman7212@gmail.com

Bishop Van I. Sharpe
Newness of Life Christian Center
P. O. Box 1462
Tarboro, N. C. 27886
(252) 641-0098
E-mail: godisable@embarqmail.com
Website: www.newnessoflifechristiancenter.org

IN REMEMBRANCE

This book is written in remembrance of the mighty men and women of God gone on before us. They died in faith and never doubted for one moment that God couldn't heal or work miracles. Their legacy of faith still lives on in us who are fighting similar battles and must be strong and courageous in the midst of the fight.

Contents

ABOUT THE AUTHOR

Bishop Van I. Sharpe is a resident and native of Tarboro, N. C. He is a graduate of Tarboro High School in Tarboro and graduated Magna Cum Laude with a B. A. degree in Mass Communications from Shaw University in Raleigh, N. C. He is the pastor and founder of Newness of Life Christian Center in Tarboro, N. C. He is married to Resunester Sharpe, and they are proud parents of one lovely daughter, Vanneika Aireesh Sharpe and one handsome grandson, Taiden Rashad Sharpe and a gorgeous granddaughter, Adaylyn Renee' Sharpe. His ministry includes pastoring, developing and overseeing leaders, flowing in the prophetic, and evangelizing in various states.

ACKNOWLEGEMENTS

God you are awesome! Thanks for inspiring me once again to pen such powerful words on the pages of this book. I know your desire is to glorify your name through all that I say and do. I give you all the glory and I pray that my faith has pleased you once again!

Special thanks to my lovely wife, Resunester Sharpe who has always exemplified faith when we had to exercise it. It is my hope that our faith will be remembered by our daughter and grandchildren.

Special thanks to my special Family! My daughter, Vanneika, my grandson, Taiden and my granddaughter, Adaylyn, my mom, Shirley Sharpe and my two sisters, Pastor Susan Sharpe and Gloria Boyd. Your prayers and love you give on a continual basis mean the world to me.

Special thanks to my brother, Bishop Ronald Wayne Sharpe and his precious wife, Marjorie for your prayers and faith that you walk in. I love you guys!

Special thanks to my brother-in-law, Frankie Reynolds for believing in the vision enough to constantly release your wife, Beverly Reynolds to help edit this book. Beverly thanks again for your efforts to make this book a priority in your life.

Special thanks to Newness of Life for being a church that believes in the authority of God's word. Where would we be if God didn't work miracles?

INTRODUCTION

(RELEASE THE POWER)

"THERE ARE ONLY TWO WAYS TO LIVE
YOUR LIFE. ONE IS AS THOUGH NOTHING
IS A MIRACLE. THE OTHER IS AS THOUGH
EVERYTHING IS A MIRACLE."

Albert Einstein

This quote made by one who many considered a genius should help us make a decision as to how you and I decide to live our lives. Albert Einstein is mentioning two extremes. If I was to error on one of the two sides, I would rather error on the side that everything is a miracle because I would hate to need one and not even believe in them.

With that being said, I do not believe that nothing is a miracle, nor do I believe that everything is a miracle. I believe that miracles are necessary when we are at our wits' end. It is usually at this time that we cry out to God and give him an opportunity to cause miracles to happen for us.

Psalm 107:27,28 *"They reel to and fro, and stagger like a drunken man, and are at their wits' end. Then they cry unto the Lord in their trouble, and he bringeth them out of their darkness."*

The word **miracle** means "an effect or extraordinary event in the physical world that surpasses all known human or natural powers and is ascribed to a supernatural cause." It is truly sad and mind boggling to meet so many skeptics and unbelievers who have decided to deny the miraculous even though the day and hour in which we live seems to require more miracles than ever. Every true man and woman of God must acknowledge that we are in need to see cancer, diabetes, arthritis, and many other diseases healed. Far too many are using pills or some other type of prescription drugs to find some form of relief. We are now finding ourselves in the midst of a generation which takes a pill to get up, a pill to stay up without pain, and a pill to go to sleep.

The Spiritual Leadership of our day needs to get desperate. We should refuse to just preach or teach without any type of demonstration of the power of God. The Apostle Paul penned these words to the Corinthian church,

> 1 Corinthians 2:4-5 *"And my speech and my preaching was not with enticing words of man's wisdom, but in demonstration of the Spirit and of power: [5] That your faith should not stand in the wisdom of men, but in the power of God."*

These are moments that are desperately crying out to the church to walk in the Supernatural Power of God. Moments like these are saying to us, "***RELEASE THE POWER***." Our response must be, "We shall and we will!"

HEARING OF FAITH

Galatians 3:5 *"He therefore that ministereth to you the Spirit, and worketh miracles among you, doeth he it by the works of the law, or by the hearing of faith?"*

There is no way that we as a nation, family, or the church can expect to see miracles without the hearing of faith. It takes faith to bring the power of God in our midst. We know that the kind of faith that we need is based on you and I hearing the word of God.

Romans 10:17 *"So then faith cometh by hearing, and hearing by the word of God."*

We who are called to preach must truly understand that in order for people to get the faith that they need in order to get the miracles that they need, people must hear faith. Preachers, called of God, have been sent with the word of faith in their heart and mouth. This good news that Jesus saves, heals, and delivers brings hope and faith alive.

Romans 10:14-16 *"How then shall they call on him in whom they have not believed? and how shall they believe in him of whom they have not heard? and how shall they hear without a preacher? [15] And how shall they preach, except they be sent? as it is written, How beautiful are the feet of them that preach the gospel of peace, and bring glad tidings of good things! [16] But they have not all obeyed the gospel. For Esaias saith, Lord, who hath believed our report?"*

These verses make us aware that the preachers report must be believed. Apostle Paul makes it clear to us by using a quote from Isaiah who asked the question, "Who hath believed our report?" Therefore, if you don't believe what the preacher is proclaiming in line with the word and the finished work of Jesus Christ, you won't have the faith to receive your miracle.

When the preacher preached the word concerning Christ's death, burial, and resurrection, you mixed your faith with that and got saved. You must now mix your faith when he or she is preaching about healing, deliverance, and what the power of God can do. God still works miracles, but his preachers must be believed. In the same way that people believe the weather man's report concerning snow, hurricanes, or storms, we must believe God's report spoken by the man or woman of God.

Hebrews 4:2 "For unto us was the gospel preached, as well as unto them: but the word preached did not profit them, not being mixed with faith in them that heard it."

This potent verse tells us the importance of hearing the word and mixing our faith with it. Moses was indeed anointed and chosen of God to bring the people out of Egypt and into the promised land. The people didn't believe the word spoken by Moses and missed out on this part of the promise. Their murmuring and complaining eventually made Moses act unbecomingly. He ended up seeing the promised land, but he never entered the promised land.

It is important to notice that a person can use their faith in one area and receive great results and operate in doubt in another area and receive nothing. Allow me to explain. There are some people who believe that God can save your soul, but refuse to believe that he will bless you financially or heal your body. These people will usually walk around saved, but they miss out on an opportunity for God to remove cancer from their bodies or bless them financially. They live on the financial level of what they can do in their own strength, which is fine when you are a multi-millionaire or a billionaire. But what about those who weren't born with a silver spoon in their mouths or their jobs are paying only two or three dollars more than minimum wage? They need to know that tithing and giving produces miracles!

Others who believe in financial miracles need to know that the same God who blesses us with financial miracles also allowed his Son, Jesus Christ to be beaten and die on the cross so we can be healed.

Isaiah 53:3-5 *"He is despised and rejected of men; a man of sorrows, and acquainted with grief: and we hid as it were our faces from him; he was despised, and we esteemed him not. [4] Surely he hath borne our griefs, and carried our sorrows: yet we did esteem him stricken, smitten of God, and afflicted. [5] But he was wounded for our transgressions, he was bruised for our iniquities: the chastisement of our peace was upon him; and with his stripes we are healed."*

There are some preachers due to ignorance or no faith in the area of healing who say that the word "healed" used in this verse doesn't apply to the healing of the physical body, but rather to the soul. However, that is absolutely not true. The word healed here is the Hebrew word "**rapha** (raw-faw)," which means to mend, to repair, to make whole, to make healthy, and to cure. It also means physician or to mend by stitching.

Based on these definitions alone, we can see that God is talking about the physical body being healed. This same Hebrew word "**rapha**" is used in the Old Testament referring to healing.

Exodus 15:26 *"And said, If thou wilt diligently hearken to the voice of the Lord thy God, and wilt do that which is right in his sight, and wilt give ear to his commandments, and keep all his statutes, I will put none of these diseases upon thee, which I have brought upon the Egyptians: for I am the Lord that healeth thee."*

Notice this verse is talking about those physical diseases that were on the Egyptians. God isn't talking about the soul or the mind in this verse. He is talking about physical or natural diseases. In fact, it is in this verse that God reveals one of his names, Jehovah Rapha (the Lord that heals). Notice he isn't the one who makes us sick. He is the great physician. He causes us to mend. He makes us whole. He cures us.

Another verse that uses this same Hebrew word "**rapha**" is found in the book of Psalms. Please notice that it is also referring to the physical diseases being removed or the body being repaired

Psalm 103:1-3 *"Bless the Lord, O my soul: and all that is within me, bless his holy*

*name. [2] Bless the Lord, O my soul, and
forget not all his benefits: [3] Who forgiveth
all thine iniquities; who healeth all thy
diseases;"*

The Psalmist is telling us why we should salute or congratulate the Lord. One of the reasons God deserves to be celebrated and we should bless him is because he continues to heal us when we face any kind of sickness in our bodies. The Hebrew word for bless is **barak** (baw-rak) which means to kneel, bow, salute, congratulate, and to thank. We thank him out of our soul because he heals our diseases. Hallelujah!

I want you to also know that the word of God never contradicts itself. The Old Testament and New Testament aren't contradictory. We just need to be taught by people who know how to rightly divide the word.

2 Timothy 2:15 *"Study to shew thyself
approved unto God, a workman that needeth
not to be ashamed, rightly dividing the word
of truth."*

Those of us who really study the word of God will notice that God establishes his word by two or more witnesses. I have given you several verses to prove that God wants you well physically. But I will go even further to prove to you that Isaiah 53:3-5 is talking about your physical healing. Look at the New Testament unveiling these verses,

Matthew 8:16-17 *"When the even was come, they brought unto him many that were possessed with devils: and he cast out the spirits with his word, and healed all that were sick: [17] That it might be fulfilled which was spoken by Esaias the prophet, saying, Himself took our infirmities, and bare our sicknesses."*

Jesus healed Peter's mother-in-law who was sick of a fever. After this was done, later in the evening people were brought to him and demons were cast out, and people were healed of sicknesses. This was a fulfillment of the words spoken by Isaiah.

The word "healed" used in verse sixteen is the Greek word **therapeuo** (ther-ap-yoo-o), which means to cure, to relieve of disease, and to restore to health. Notice Jesus took away their sicknesses. He made them whole. Hallelujah!

The last and final scripture that unveils the words spoken by Isaiah that I wish to point out is found in the book of First Peter.

> 1 Peter 2:24 *"Who his own self bare our sins in his own body on the tree, that we, being dead to sins, should live unto righteousness: by whose stripes ye were healed."*

The Greek word "healed" used in this verse is **iaomai** (ee-ah'-om-ahee), which means to cure, to make whole, and to free from error or sin. It means "to bring about one's salvation." In other words this Greek word is covering everything. Jesus' stripes freed us from sin and disease. The cross took care of it all. Hallelujah!

The Bible teaches us that sin brought sickness and death on the scene for mankind. If the first Adam would have never sinned, man (male and female) wouldn't have had to die. Jesus defeated death and brought resurrection. He brought eternal life.

1 Corinthians 15:21 *"For since by man came death, by man came also the resurrection of the dead."*

The point I am seeking to make is that we need to hear the word of faith to be saved, healed, and prosper financially. The preaching of the word of faith allows the word to get in the right places. It allows the word to get in the hearts and mouths of men.

Mark 16:20 *"And they went forth, and preached every where, the Lord working with them, and confirming the word with signs following. Amen."*

Romans 10:8 *"But what saith it? The word is nigh thee, even in thy mouth, and in thy heart: that is, the word of faith, which we preach;"*

ENTER IN

Hebrews 4:1 *"Let us therefore fear, lest, a promise being left us of entering into his rest, any of you should seem to come short of it."*

Hebrews 4:6 *"Seeing therefore it remaineth that some must enter therein, and they to whom it was first preached entered not in because of unbelief:"*

The only reason why the children of Israel didn't enter into the promise land was because of unbelief. Their unbelief caused them to live a defeated life. It caused them to walk in a way offensive to God. This was a promise that they should have received, but doubt was in their hearts and ruined it for them.

2 Corinthians 1:20 *"For all the promises of God in him are yea, and in him Amen, unto the glory of God by us."*

Jesus came to make all the promises of God available to us. We should seek to receive all of them, especially since in Christ we have a "yes" to all of them. They had the promise preached to them and didn't believe it, but now it is our turn. We must choose to believe and receive miracle after miracle! This is what you and I should stay excited about experiencing. When the natural has been exhausted, we should be aware that miracles still exist to make the impossible possible. Yes, I still believe in miracles. I believe that you and I will never reach our destiny without having to trust God for miracles. The question is, "Are you ready to enter in?"

Luke 5:12-13 *"And it came to pass, when he was in a certain city, behold a man full of leprosy: who seeing Jesus fell on his face, and besought him, saying, Lord, if thou wilt, thou canst make me clean. [13] And he put forth his hand, and touched him, saying, I will: be thou clean. And immediately the leprosy departed from him."*

We must not allow others who don't believe in miracles or who don't need a miracle to pollute our hearts with their critical or cynical attitudes. I love a quote made by Dr. I. V. Hillard many years ago. He said, "Because you might have arrived at a **no need state** through some unintentional natural process doesn't give you the right to deny me the clearly revealed spiritual biblical plan of God to elevate me and others to the same **no need state**."

In other words, he was saying that just because some people never had to use their faith for their finances or a healing in their body, it doesn't mean you can't use your faith in these areas. Some people have been raised in a family that knew how to properly manage their finances. They may have been born in a wealthy household. Therefore, the need to trust God for their finances has never been exercised thus far.

Some people have exercised properly and eaten the proper foods and thus far have never had to use their faith for the healing of their body. The minor ailments that they have encountered have been able to be diagnosed and rectified by a doctor.

Neither case should cause you not to put your faith to work if you are in need of the supernatural. I believe that many who may not need a miracle now will eventually before this life is over need a miracle for themselves or someone that they love dearly.

You can't let the doubters or skeptics shut you out of the promised land. You must go for your own advantage. The promises are sure to all the seed of Abraham, and since you belong to Jesus Christ that includes you.

Romans 4:16 *"Therefore it is of faith, that it might be by grace; to the end the promise might be sure to all the seed; not to that only which is of the law, but to that which is of the faith of Abraham; who is the father of us all"*

Galatians 3:29 *"And if ye be Christ's, then are ye Abraham's seed, and heirs according to the promise."*

We must know that who we are matters to God. He wants all of us to be born into the family of God through faith. Once we become Abraham's seed by faith, we have a right to be free from anything that Satan tries to bind or keep us bound with.

Luke 13:16 *"And ought not this woman, being a daughter of Abraham, whom Satan hath bound, lo, these eighteen years, be loosed from this bond on the Sabbath day?"*

Notice this woman had an infirmity for eighteen years, but as the seed of Abraham, she had the right to be free. Jesus knew and understood the covenant that God the Father had made with Abraham. He knew that God had promised to bless Abraham and his seed. He knew this woman being bowed together and not being able to lift up herself was not a blessing.

You must know that poverty and sickness are not blessings. Anything that limits your ability to have a healthy and productive life is not a blessing. Anger, doubt, and procrastination try to keep us out of a multitude of things that we are entitled to, but we need to reach out and grab them because of Jesus Christ.

I must warn you and make you aware that everyone will not be happy when you are healed or blessed. But I advise you to ignore them and possess the good word of his promise. Jesus knew his assignment was to heal this woman. He didn't allow the indignation of the ruler of the synagogue to hinder him.

Jesus knew the woman had been in that condition long enough, and it was time to set her free. As a man of God, I say to you that it is time for you to be free from the oppression of the devil or Satan. That sickness must leave your body or the body of your loved one. It must go now in the name of Jesus! Enter into Healing Now!

FAITH IN THE BLOOD OF JESUS

The worst thing we can do as men and women of God is allow the devil to take us away from the victory that we have through the blood of Jesus. Anyone who is a believer must know and understand the Passover. We all know that the children of Israel in the Old Testament had to take a lamb for their houses to protect everything inside their houses. The lamb had to be a male without blemish. It was to be killed in the evening and the blood of the lamb was to be stricken on the two sides of the posts of the house and on the upper door posts of the house. The Israelites were to roast the flesh in the night with fire and eat it with unleavened bread.

Exodus 12:3-13 *"Speak ye unto all the congregation of Israel, saying, In the tenth day of this month they shall take to them every man a lamb, according to the house of their fathers, a lamb for an house: [4] And if the household be too little for the lamb, let him and his neighbor next unto his house take it according to the number of the souls; every man according to his eating shall make your count for the lamb. [5] Your lamb shall be without blemish, a male of the first year: ye shall take it out from the sheep, or from the goats: [6] And ye shall keep it up until the fourteenth day of the same month: and the whole assembly of the congregation of Israel shall kill it in the evening. [7] And they shall take of the blood, and strike it on the two side posts and on the upper door post of the houses, wherein they shall eat it. [8] And they shall eat the flesh in that night, roast with fire, and unleavened bread; and with bitter herbs they shall eat it. [10] And ye shall let nothing of it remain until the morning; and that which remaineth of it until the morning, ye shall burn with fire. [11] And thus shall ye eat it; with your loins girded, your shoes on your feet, and your staff in your hand; and ye shall eat it in haste: it is the Lord's passover. [12] For I will pass through the land of Egypt this night, and will smite all the firstborn in the land of Egypt, both man and beast; and against all the gods of Egypt I will execute judgement: I am the Lord. [13] And the blood shall be to you for a token upon the houses where ye are: and when I see the blood, I will pass over you, and the plague shall not be upon you to destroy you, when I smite the land of Egypt."*

These verses show us that it was the blood of a male lamb without blemish that saved Israel from the plague. Without the blood of the Lamb the first born of the Israelites would have died, but because of the blood God passed over their houses. The New Testament tells us that Jesus is our Passover. He is the male Lamb that was slain. John the Baptist saw him as the Lamb and yelled out to everyone that was able to hear him,

John 1:29 *"The next day John seeth Jesus coming unto him, and saith, Behold the Lamb of God, which taketh away the sin of the world."*

John 1:36 *"And looking upon Jesus as he walked, he saith, Behold the Lamb of God!"*

Two disciples of John the Baptist heard him utter these words and immediately left him and began to follow Jesus. We must understand that the Lamb is the one we should follow and believe on today. Jesus shed his blood to keep us from eternal damnation. He is our Passover.

> I Corinthians 5:7 *"Purge out therefore the old leaven, that ye may be a new lump, as ye are unleavened. For even Christ our Passover is sacrificed for us:"*

Our faith must be applied in the blood of Jesus the same way Moses put his faith in the blood of the lamb. He believed in that sprinkled blood and you and I must believe in the blood of Jesus.

> Hebrews 11:28 *"Through faith he kept the passover, and the sprinkling of blood, lest he that destroyed the firstborn should touch them."*

I remind you that none of them were hurt because of their faith in the blood of an animal. Surely, we should know that if we have faith in the blood of Jesus Christ, we will be kept from the plagues of our day. It is the sprinkling of the blood of Jesus that makes the difference.

There is no way that God will respect and honor the blood of lambs, goats, and bulls used in the Old Testament more than he will the blood of his only begotten Son, Jesus Christ. The blood of Jesus Christ cleanses us and sanctifies us from all unrighteousness! The blood of bulls and goats never took away sins.

> Hebrews 10:1-4 *"For the law having a shadow of good things to come, and not the very image of the things, can never with those sacrifices which they offered year by year continually make the comers thereunto perfect. [2] For then would they not have ceased to be offered? because that the worshippers once purged should have no more conscience of sins. [3] But in those sacrifices there is a remembrance again made of sins every year. [4] For it is not possible that the blood of bulls and goats should take away sins."*

Jesus offered up himself one time, and we are made perfect through his blood. His blood does more for us. It not only sanctifies us, but it purged our conscience from dead works.

Hebrews 9:13,14 *"For if the blood of bulls and of goats, and the ashes of an heifer sprinkling the unclean, sanctifieth to the purifying of the flesh: How much more shall the blood of Christ, who through the eternal Spirit offered himself without spot to God, purge your conscience from dead works to serve the living God?"*

Moses obeyed God and sprinkled the book of the law, the people, the tabernacle, and all the vessels of the ministry. His faith was in the blood. The blood was powerful and important. The blood was sprinkled on the testament, the people, the tabernacle, and the vessels of the ministry.

Hebrew 9:19-22 *"For when Moses had spoken every precept to all the people according to the law, he took the blood of calves and of goats, with water, and scarlet wool, and hyssop, and sprinkled both the book, and all the people, [20] Saying, This is the blood of the testament which God hath enjoined unto you. [21] Moreover he sprinkled with blood both the tabernacle, and all the vessels of the ministry. [22] And almost all things are by the law purged with blood; and without shedding of blood is no remission."*

Jesus shed his blood for us and his blood obtained eternal redemption for us. His blood makes it possible for us to go beyond the veil and get a private personal audience with God Almighty. We can now come boldly to the throne of grace.

Hebrews 10:19 *"Having therefore, brethren, boldness to enter into the holiest by the blood of Jesus,"*

The blood of Jesus also seals and ratifies the New Covenant. The sufferings of Jesus should never be forgotten. His body was beaten and his blood was shed, and we should remember that the same night when Judas betrayed Jesus, he had a supper with them. It is referred to as "The Last Supper." We who are in the body of Christ today call it "Holy Communion."

Luke 22:20 *"Likewise also the cup after supper, saying, this cup is the new testament in my blood, which is shed for you."*

I Corinthians 10:16 *"The cup of blessing which we bless, is it not the communion of the blood of Christ? The bread which we break, is it not the communion of the body of Christ?"*

I Corinthians 11:23-25 *"For I received of the Lord that which also I delivered unto you, That the Lord Jesus the same night in which he was betrayed took bread: [24] And when he had given thanks, he brake it, and said, Take eat: this is my body, which is broken for you: this do in remembrance of me. [25] After the same manner also he took the cup, when he had supped, saying, This cup is the new testament in my blood: this do ye, as oft as ye drink it, in remembrance of me."*

Eating and drinking of this bread and cup unworthily causes a person to eat and drink damnation to himself. In fact, the Apostle Paul penned that many of the saints were weak, sickly, and dead because they had not properly examined themselves. They had not properly discerned the Lord's body. Notice these verses of scripture,

1 Corinthians 11:29, 30 *"For he that eateth and drinketh unworthily, eateth and drinketh damnation to himself, not discerning the Lord's body. [30] For this cause many are weak and sickly among you, and many sleep."*

If not properly discerning, the Lord's body can cause sickness and death, then discerning the Lord's body can cause healing and life. We have been redeemed by the blood from our old empty lifestyle. This redemption wasn't paid for with money, but with something more precious than money. It took the blood of the Lamb to redeem you and I. We are God's elect because of the blood of Jesus!

I Peter 1:18,19 *"Forasmuch as ye know that ye were not redeemed with corruptible things, as silver and gold, from your vain conversation received by tradition from your father; [19] But with the precious blood of Christ, as of a lamb without blemish and without spot:"*

1 Peter 1:2 *"Elect according to the foreknowledge of God the Father, through sanctification of the Spirit, unto obedience*

and sprinkling of the blood of Jesus Christ:
Grace unto you, and peace, be multiplied."

God didn't buy us to lose us. He bought us to take us into his precious promises. This includes healing. Jesus, through his blood, did not set into motion a temporary covenant. The blood of Jesus was the blood of an everlasting covenant.

Hebrews 13:20 *"Now the God of peace, that brought again from the dead our Lord Jesus, that great shepherd of the sheep, through the blood of the everlasting covenant."*

The diseases that are in the earth today are still no match for the blood of our Lord Jesus. These diseases may have more sophisticated names and may seem to be more than some of our medical technology, but the blood will never lose its power. It is still potent enough to be recognized by our Heavenly Father, and it still is recognized by the devil.

No matter what accusations that the accuser is trying to use against you to try to make you think you deserve to be sick, you must use the blood of Jesus against him. Tell the devil that the blood is stronger than your past, present, or future sins. It has entitled you to win and overcome! It is time to Plead the Blood! I still believe that there is still wonder working power in the Precious Blood of the Lamb.

> Revelation 12:10,11 *"And I heard a loud voice saying in heaven, Now is come salvation, and strength, and the kingdom of our God, and the power of his Christ: for the accuser of our brethren is cast down, which accused them before our God day and night. [11] And they overcame him by the blood of the Lamb, and by the word of their testimony; and they loved not their lives unto the death."*

FAITH IN THE NAME OF JESUS

John 14:13-14 "And whatsoever ye shall ask in my name, that will I do, that the Father may be glorified in the Son. [14] If ye shall ask any thing in my name, I will do it."

Acts 3:6-8,16 "Then Peter said, Silver and gold have I none; but such as I have give I thee: In the name of Jesus Christ of Nazareth rise up and walk. [7] And he took him by the right hand, and lifted him up: and immediately his feet and ankle bones received strength. [8] And he leaping up stood, and walked, and entered with them into the temple, walking, and leaping, and praising God. [16] And his name through faith in his name hath made this man strong, whom ye see and know: yea, the faith which is by him hath given him this perfect soundness in the presence of you all."

Jesus wanted his disciples to know the authority of the name of Jesus in the earth. He wanted those that he chose to walk in faith in the name of Jesus. It is the most powerful name in the earth and in heaven. It is the only name that man can be saved by. I remember some powerful words a great Bible scholar who preached for me many years ago told me. He said, "When you get faith in his name like you've got faith in your own name, you will see more miracles." He went on to say that the difference between people who see healing miracles in their ministry more than you is that they've developed more faith in the name of Jesus than you. These words were profound and would become a catalyst to train me to walk in the power of the supernatural on a new level. He told me that the apostles put their faith in the name of Jesus.

Notice the Apostle Peter doesn't credit his holiness or power for healing the lame man at the gate called Beautiful. This man had never walked before in his life, but through the use of the name of Jesus Christ, the man walks, leaps, and praises God. Peter made them aware of the fact that God had glorified his Son Jesus. He told them that the name of Jesus and faith in the name of Jesus had made the man strong.

We can help someone's life flourish and blossom if we learn to have faith in the name of Jesus. When the Bishop told me those potent words, I thought about growing up in the projects. Everyone in the projects that I grew up in as a little boy seemed like family. We could leave our apartments with the screen door unlocked, and no one would rob our house or bother anything in our place. If one person had sugar or salt, everyone had sugar or salt because we could go borrow some from them.

I remember my father would send me to go get a cigarette or something from his friends who lived in the projects. I remember I would say to them, "My dad wants you to send him a cigarette." The next question would be "Who is your daddy" or "What is your daddy's name?" As soon as I would say, "Eddie Frank Sharpe," they would go get the cigarette immediately. I was never turned down once I would tell his name.

The same was true when my mother would send me or my brother to get some sugar or salt from one of the women living in the projects. As soon as I would tell them that my mother was "Shirley Mae Sharpe," these women would give it to me. My dad and my mom knew that their names would cause the item to be released based on their names, which carried weight among those who heard their names mentioned.

The name of Jesus carries that type of weight and more. Jesus knows that when his disciples go out using his name, the Father will release the miracle. The devil has to turn people loose when we have faith in the name of Jesus.

Bishop Johnson also told me something else that really blew me out of the water. He said that when you really start releasing your faith in his name enough times, you will be able to exercise the authority of the name of Jesus without even saying his name. As a young pastor back then, I was blown away, and I said, "Prove that." He took me to the story of the man who heard the Apostle Paul preach. Notice these verses,

Acts 14:9,10 *"The same heard Paul speak: who stedfastly beholding him, and perceiving that he had faith to be healed, [10] Said with a loud voice, Stand with a loud voice, Stand upright on thy feet. And he leaped and walked."*

The Apostle Paul didn't tell the man to stand upright in Jesus' name. He had so much faith in the name that the Heavenly Father knew he was telling the man to do it in Jesus' name and so did the devil. Sickness turned the man loose without Paul using the name verbally. Yet, we know the man was healed by the authority of the name of Jesus.

Let me explain it even better by the example I gave you earlier with my dad and mom. You see after my brother and I had borrowed these items (cigarettes, sugar, salt, detergent) from the neighbors in the projects a few times, they knew what our faces looked like. They knew our parents, but now they knew us as their children. Therefore, when we would go ask to borrow the items, we would say, "Our dad wants to borrow a cigarette" or "Our mom wants to borrow a cup of sugar." We never had to say their names again because it was understood whose names we were coming in.

All we need to do is use the name of Jesus every time sickness and disease lifts its ugly head until eventually every devil knows that we are commanding sickness to go in Jesus' name even though we never said it. Not only did the Apostle Paul function like this, but so did the Apostle Peter. Peter even had so much faith in the authority of the name that he was sent in that he even raised the dead without ever saying in the name of Jesus.

> Acts 9:40 *"But Peter put them all forth, and kneeled down, and prayed; and turning him to the body said, Tabitha, arise. And she opened her eyes: and when she saw Peter, she sat up."*

Notice a woman was sick and died. The people had washed her body and laid her in the upper chamber, but Peter had his faith in the power of the name of Jesus. He knew that Jesus had told him to go and use the name of Jesus to cast out devils, heal the sick, and raise the dead. In other words, they were to go as his representatives or ambassadors.

They were to get so much faith in his name that they were never to be intimidated by the disease. They were to take on the character and nature of that name to the point it was just like Jesus was there in the person of his disciples. This takes faith and time to get to this level, but if you see chosen vessels walk in this level of authority and you begin to exercise your authority time and time again, you will be able to function on this level.

Peter never said, "Arise in Jesus' name." He just looked at the body and said, "Tabitha arise." The woman opened her eyes and sat up. This type of authority allows people to know that the kingdom of God is at hand.

> Matthew 10:7,8 *"And as ye go, preach, saying, The kingdom of heaven is at hand. Heal the sick, cleanse the lepers, raise the dead, cast out devils: freely ye have received, freely give."*

Preaching that the kingdom of God is at hand is incomplete without demonstrating the authority of the name of Jesus Christ. The word **authority** means delegated power. It means the right to control, command, or determine. Authority is persuasive force. Just like a policeman has been given authority to stop traffic or crooks, we have been given authority to be used against the devil and his works.

> Luke 9:1,2 *"Then he called his twelve disciples together, and gave them power and authority over all devils, and to cure diseases. [2] And he sent them to preach the kingdom of God, and to heal the sick."*

We as new creations are called to share authority with Christ. He made us to sit together with him in heavenly places. This is a **supernatural place** in the spirit realm at the right hand of God. This place of rulership is respected by the world of demons and sickness. It is a lofty place. Jesus and his church have been made to sit in the heavenly places now that Christ has been raised from the dead. It is far above the demonic and sickness world.

> Ephesians 1:21 *"Far above all principality, and power, and might, and dominion, and every name that is named, not only in this world, but also in that which is to come:"*

God has put all things under the feet of Jesus and made him to be head over the church. We should have faith in his name to know that we will receive what we ask in his name. In the same way that as a child I didn't expect my neighbors to deny my father or mother, I don't expect my Heavenly Father to deny my request in his Son's name. It is a done deal! You can command cancer to leave, Aids to leave, and any other disease. The name of Jesus Christ is far above these names. Your faith in the name of Jesus will make you whole from the crown of your head to the soles of your feet!

RELEASING THE POWER THROUGH SPEECH AND TOUCH

Ephesians 3:20 *"Now unto him that is able to do exceeding abundantly above all that we ask or think, according to the power that worketh in us,"*

The word "power" used in this verse is the Greek word **dynamis** (doo-na-mis), which means force, ability, strength, abundance, and mighty work. This word dynamis means inherent power. It is the power that belongs to riches and wealth. It is the power that performs miracles. It is the type of power that rests upon armies or hosts.

The Apostle Paul tells us that this type of miraculous power is in us to do above what we can imagine or think. This supernatural power makes things happen that exceed our wildest dreams. This power of the Holy Spirit enables us to carry out the purpose of the Father.

> John 14:12-14,16 *"Verily, verily, I say unto you, He that believeth on me, the works that I do shall he do also; and greater works than these shall he do; because I go unto my Father. [13] And whatsoever ye shall ask in my name, that will I do, that the Father may be glorified in the Son. [14], I will do it. [16] And If ye shall ask any thing in my name I will pray the Father, and he shall give you another Comforter, that he may abide with you for ever;"*

> EPHESIANS 3:20 AMP *"Now to Him who is able to [carry out His purpose and] do superabundantly more than all that we dare ask or think [infinitely beyond our greatest prayers, hopes, or dreams], according to His power that is at work within us,"*

We must recognize that the purpose of God can never be carried out in its fullness without miracles. I believe God will lead us in a way that will cause others to not give honor and glory to our intellect, but give honor and glory to the Miraculous Power of God!

Once we put our faith in the blood of Jesus and faith in the name of Jesus, we must release the power of God like Jesus and his disciples did when they were in the earth. They released their faith in two basic ways that I would like to discuss in this book. The first way is by speaking the word. Jesus and his disciples would just declare what they wanted people who were sick to do, or they would command the disease to depart. The people and the sickness obeyed.

Those of us who are born of God must know that we have power to speak the word and see results. We don't have to always touch the sick person, but we can with our words command the disease to depart. We can tell a person to stand who has never walked or command them to move their arm or stretch it out. Every time we do it, we are operating in our authority as kings.

Ecclesiastes 8:4 *"Where the word of a king is, there is power: and who may say unto him, What doest thou?"*

A king knows that when he speaks, results take place. Jesus is the King of kings and when he walked this earth, he was fully aware that when he spoke the wind, sea, fish, people, and diseases obeyed. The disciples who walked with Jesus in his earthly ministry saw this demonstrated. After his death and resurrection took place, the disciples then went forth and watched God confirm his word through them in the same manner.

Mark 16:20 *"And they went forth, and preached every where, the Lord working with them, and confirming the word with signs following. Amen."*

Miracles both in the area of diseases and finances should be expected once we release our faith through words. When you have authority, you don't have to be in the same place as others. You can send your word to a place and get dynamic results.

Psalm 107:20 *"He sent his word, and healed them, and delivered them from their destructions."*

The Bible tells us the story of a centurion who understood that Jesus could be in one place and speak his word in another place, and people could be healed by faith in that word. He knew it could happen because he was a man under authority. He had soldiers under his authority, and he would tell them to go, and they would go, or he would tell them to come, and they would come. His type of faith was pleasing to Jesus, and his servant was able to be healed without Jesus' physical touch but by the spoken word.

> Matthew 8:8,13 *"The centurion answered and said, Lord, I am not worthy that thou shouldest come under my roof: but speak the word only, and my servant shall be healed. [13] and Jesus said unto the centurion, Go thou way; and as thou hast believed, so be it unto thee. And his servant was healed in the selfsame hour."*

I can't tell you how many times that I've seen different saints or people tell me about someone who is suffering in their bodies. We speak the word, and their loved one recovers immediately. I've seen operations canceled because the doctors can't find the disease, or the person gets up out of bed during the same hour.

Notice Jesus didn't pray. He spoke the word. The centurion didn't tell Jesus to pray. He told Jesus to speak the word. Many believers pray when they should just speak the word. They should release their faith in the words that they utter. Let's look at another example of Jesus releasing his faith through his words.

Mark 3:1-5 *"And he entered again into the synagogue; and there was a man there which had a withered hand. [2] And they watched him, whether he would heal him on the sabbath day; that they might accuse him. [3] And he saith unto the man which had the withered hand, Stand forth. [4] And he saith unto them, Is it lawful to do good on the sabbath days, or to do evil? to save life, or to kill? But they held their peace. [5] And when he had looked round about on them with anger, being grieved for the hardness of their hearts, he saith unto the man, Stretch forth thine hand. And he stretched it out: and his hand was restored whole as the other."*

In this story of the man with a withered hand, please notice that Jesus spoke to the man. He told the man to "Stand forth." Then he told the man to stretch forth his hand. The man obeyed the words of Jesus, and his hand was restored. Again we see Jesus didn't pray for the man's hand or the man. He told the man what he wanted him to do. Jesus was releasing his faith, and he gave the man a chance to release his faith. They both did, and the miracle took place. Notice that Jesus didn't waste time telling God the situation of the man. He released his faith by telling the man what he wanted done.

I am not teaching you to tell God to go by the rest home or stop by the hospital. I am telling you to learn how to release your faith by speaking the word and watch results without you being there physically or ever touching the sick person. I will show you another example of Jesus doing this type of thing. It is the story of a woman who had a daughter grievously vexed of a devil. This woman wanted her daughter set free or delivered. She was a Gentile, but she knew that Jesus could deliver her daughter without ever touching her. Her faith caused her daughter to be made whole.

> Matthew 15:22-28 *"And, behold, a woman of Canaan came out of the same coasts, and cried unto him, saying, Have mercy on me, O Lord, thou Son of David; my daughter is grievously vexed with a devil. [23] But he answered her not a word. And his disciples came and besought him, saying, Send her away; for she crieth after us. [24] But he answered and said, I am not sent but unto the lost sheep of the house of Israel. [25] Then came she and worshipped him, saying, Lord, help me. [26] But he answered and said, It is not meet to take the children's bread, and to cast it to dogs. [27] And she said, Truth, Lord: yet the dogs eat of the crumbs which fall from their masters' table. [28] Then Jesus answered and said unto her, O woman, great is thy faith: be it unto thee even as thou wilt. And her daughter was made whole from that very hour."*

The same way Jesus didn't have to touch people neither did his Apostles. They saw people healed and set free from diseases by speaking the word.

Acts 9:33,34 *"And there he found a certain man named Aeneas, which had kept his bed eight years, and was sick of the palsy. And Peter said unto him, Aeneas, Jesus Christ maketh thee whole: arise, and make thy bed. And he arose immediately."*

In these verses we see the Apostle Peter releasing his faith to tell the man to arise, and we see the man releasing his faith and getting up immediately. Aeneas didn't try to explain to Peter that he had been in his bed for eight years because it doesn't matter when you release your faith in the spoken word. Whatever disease has tried to hold you must let you go because I command you to "Arise!"

The Apostle Paul saw a man who was impotent in his feet, having been crippled from his mother's womb. The man had never walked before. He heard Paul preach, and the man had faith to be healed. Paul told him to stand upright, and the man leaped and walked.

Acts 14:9,10 *"The same heard Paul speak: who stedfastly beholding him, and perceiving*

*that he had faith to be healed, [10] Said with
a loud voice, Stand upright on thy feet. And
he leaped and walked."*

The second way that we release our faith
in the power of God to heal is by touch or
laying on of hands. Jesus and his disciples
touched people and saw them healed. Jesus
touched a leper and cleansed him.

Matthew 8:2,3 *"And, behold there came a
leper and worshipped him, saying, Lord, if
thou wilt, thou canst make me clean. [3] And
Jesus put forth his hand, and touched him,
saying, I will; be thou clean. And immediately
his leprosy was cleansed."*

Jesus wasn't afraid of catching the disease.
He believed people would receive healing
through his touch. He also touched Peter's
wife's mother who was sick of a fever.

Matthew 8:14,15 *"And when Jesus was come
into Peter's house, he saw his wife's mother
laid, and sick of a fever. [15] And he touched
her hand, and the fever left her: and she
arose, and ministered unto them.*

A woman having an issue of blood twelve years came behind Jesus and touched the hem of his garment and immediately was made whole. Jesus perceived that virtue was gone out of him and asked, "Who touched me?" The woman saw that she was not hid and declared before all the people that she had touched him. Then Jesus credited her faith.

Luke 8:48 *"And he said unto her, Daughter, be of good comfort: thy faith hath made thee whole; go in peace."*

Notice her faith was released when she touched the border of his garment. She believed when she touched him something supernatural would happen. She had faith for a miracle. Also, the Bible tells us of a whole multitude coming to Jesus believing that they would be healed through touching him. Their faith was released as they touched him, and all of them were healed.

Luke 6:19 *"And the whole multitude sought to touch him: for there went virtue out of him, and healed them all."*

The same way these people touched the garment of Jesus and received miracles, God worked special miracles through the Apostle Paul. The sick were healed by touching his handkerchiefs and aprons.

> Acts 19:11,12 *"And God wrought special miracles by the hands of Paul: [12] So that from his body were brought unto the sick handkerchiefs or aprons, and the diseases departed from them, and the evil spirits went out of them."*

Jesus gave his disciples power or authority over sickness and disease, which they exercised through anointing them with oil and laying hands on them. They didn't just preach, but they knew people were in need of miracles. The people needed to be cured of their diseases.

> Mark 6:12,13 *"And they went out, and preached that men should repent. [13] And they cast out many devils, and anointed with oil many that were sick, and healed them."*

The same way the disciples operated in this type of authority and power so should every believer and the elders of churches. We must not just leave it up to one man or one woman when we as believers in the Lord Jesus Christ have power. The Holy Ghost was given so that we would receive power. The power is for healing the sick and casting out devils.

> Mark 16:18 *"...they shall lay hands on the sick, and they shall recover."*

> James 5:14,15 *"Is any sick among you? let him call for the elders of the church; and let them pray over him, anointing him with oil in the name of the Lord: [15] And the prayer of faith shall save the sick, and the Lord shall raise him up; and if he have committed sins, they shall be forgiven him."*

We must notice that the type of disease doesn't matter. It still must depart, and healing will take place when we lay hands on the sick. The disease will leave the sick now in the same way that diseases left when Jesus laid his hands on them and divers diseases left.

Luke 4:40 *"Now when the sun was setting, all they that had any sick with divers diseases brought them unto him; and he laid his hands on every one of them, and healed them."*

Those of us who are full of compassion should want to do more than just preach the gospel to the sick. We should want to see them healed. We should be ready and willing to mix our faith with theirs and touch them. When I pray for the sick, I like to say as I pray for them, "Be healed from the crown of your head to the soles of your feet." My faith is released as I say those powerful words.

Again I remind you that these are two powerful ways that we release our faith. We receive miracles according to our faith. Jesus asked two blind men who followed him and cried out to him, "Believe ye that I am able to do this?" They told Jesus, "Yea, Lord." Notice what happened next,

Matthew 9:29 *"Then touched he their eyes, saying, According to your faith be it unto you."*

Jesus didn't say according to his power even though his power was released. He told them according to their faith. He touched their eyes knowing that their faith would be released and a miracle would be wrought.

APPROVED OF GOD

Acts 2:22 *"Ye men of Israel, hear these words; Jesus of Nazareth, a man approved of God among you by miracles and wonders and signs, which God did by him in the midst of you, as ye yourselves also know:"*

It is important to note that Jesus wasn't chasing titles, but titles were chasing him. His real approval of who he was as a man sent from God was due to signs and wonders. Our Heavenly Father showed that he had sent him. The Greek word for "approved" used in this sentence is **apodeiknymi** (ap-od-ike-noo-mee), which means to show off, to exhibit, to expose into view, to point out, and to demonstrate.

Acts 2:22 Amplified *"You men of Israel, listen to what I have to say: Jesus of Nazareth, a Man accredited and pointed out and shown forth and commended and attested to you by god by the mighty works and [the power of performing] wonders and signs which God worked through Him [right] in your midst, as you yourselves know-"*

In other words, God was publicly endorsing Jesus by doing miracles, wonders, and signs. God was arguing his case against any skeptics that Jesus was sent. This is why Jesus told the skeptics on one occasion to believe on him for the very work's sake. Listen at what he told those who thought he was guilty of blasphemy,

John 10:37,38 *"If I do not the works of my Father me not. [38] But if I do, though ye believe not me, believe the works: that ye may know, and believe, that the Father is in me, and I in him."*

I believe that God is still using a demonstration of his power to point out to skeptics today that he has sent us. These are the infallible proofs that can't be denied by those who believe we are not sent by God. Listen at the words penned by the Apostle Paul,

2 Corinthians 12:12 *"Truly the signs of an apostle were wrought among you in all patience, in signs, and wonders, and mighty deeds."*

Notice Paul is telling us that his apostleship was approved by God. It was approved by miracles, signs, and wonders. His apostleship was approved by patience and mighty deeds. In other words, he didn't just say he was an apostle without God exhibiting it. God pointed out Paul by the mighty works.

The word "apostle" in the New Testament is the Greek masculine noun **apostolos** (ap-os'-tol-os), which means an ambassador of the Gospel; a commissioner of Christ, a delegate, one sent forth with orders. It means sent with authority or miraculous power. These definitions alone tell us that with the title apostle should be mighty miracles.

The word "sent" used in the New Testament is the Greek verb **apostello** (ap-os-tel'-lo), which means set apart and to order (one) to go to a place appointed. It means sent out on a mission.

Those of us who are sent by God should be willing and ready to pray for the sick. Our compassion moves us to touch them or speak the word that will set the captive free. We have been set apart by God and appointed to live in certain cities and communities with the deliverance necessary to make the sick whole. You might not be an apostle in title, but you are God's representative. He has sent you with his authority.

> John 6:28,29 *"Then said they unto him, What shall we do, that we might work the works of God? [29] Jesus answered and said unto them, This is the work of God, that ye believe on him whom he hath sent."*

Jesus is telling us how important it is that we believe on him. Why? It is because Jesus was sent by God, which meant that he had the deliverance that the people needed. The same is true for you and I. People must believe that God sent us to receive the miracles they are standing in need of. In the Old Testament, God told Moses to tell Pharaoh who sent him.

> Exodus 3:14 *"And God said unto Moses, I AM THAT I AM: and he said, Thus shalt thou say*

*unto the children of Israel, I AM hath sent me
unto you."*

You must know that God who sent you gave you enough authority to defeat the power of darkness. Those who receive you are receiving the one who sent you and those who reject you are rejecting the one who sent you. You have God's approval through signs, wonders, and miracles.

Mark 9:37 *"Whosoever shall receive one of such children in my name, receiveth me: and whosoever shall receive me, receiveth not me, but him that sent me."*

I wish to make you aware of the fact that those who don't know the one who sent you will persecute you. Jesus made his disciples aware of this, and I will not be doing my job as a man of God if I didn't put you on notice as well. People who have no intimate relationship with God will think you are doing what you do in your own name and authority. They will resist, fight, and resent you instead of receiving you.

John 15:21 *"But all these things will they do unto you for my name's sake, because they know not him that sent me."*

I will expound more about being sent in my upcoming book written to Ministers. I think there is so much that needs to be said, but since this book is to help you build your faith in miracles, the time is not appropriate to elaborate. God has allowed you to read this book to know that you have Satan's eviction papers, and it is time to tell him, "To Go!"

BREAKING THE OPPRESSION OF SATAN

The word devil is the Greek word "**diabolos**," which means "One who comes to divide or slander." The word Satan is the Greek word "**Satanas**," which means "One who opposes vision and purpose." Two of the biggest ways of limiting people in their purpose is to keep them sick and keep them broke (living in poverty and lack).

Acts 10:38 *"How God anointed Jesus of Nazareth with the Holy Ghost and power: who went about doing good, and healing all that were oppressed of the devil; for God was with him."*

Matthew 8:16 *"When the even was come, they brought unto him many that were possessed with devils: and he cast out the spirits with his word, and healed all that were sick."*

Matthew 10:1 *"And when he had called unto him his twelve disciples, he gave them power against unclean spirits, to cast them out, and to heal all manner of sickness and all manner of disease."*

These three powerful verses reveal to us that Jesus as well as his disciples demonstrated power over the devil and his works. They broke the oppression of Satan off the lives of those who were bound. Neither Jesus nor his disciples tolerated the devil oppressing people with sickness and disease. They healed them all.

The word "oppression" used in Acts 10:38 is the Greek word **katadynasteuo**, which means "to exercise harsh control over one, to exercise dominion against, and to use one's power against one." The devil wants to keep his harsh control over the lives of people month after month and year after year, but Jesus wants it to stop today!

Jesus healed all manner of sickness and diseases and the disciples did the same. Now it is our turn to get the devil out of the way.

We have been given power over all the power of the enemy.

> Luke 10:19 *"Behold, I give unto you power to tread on serpents and scorpions, and over all the power of the enemy: and nothing shall by any means hurt you."*

There are those who speak like natural men who refuse to even address the havoc that Satan has wrought through poverty. He has tried to totally wipe out the lives of people through shortage and lack. God's will is prosperity for you and I, and he will indeed intervene and destroy that cycle in your life through miracles. The turning of the water to wine at the wedding was a financial miracle (John 2:7-11). Jesus took that which didn't cost (water) and created that which did cost (wine).

Jesus also shows us that God will give you financial miracles when the people came to Peter came to receive money to pay their taxes. This was a great financial miracle because it had to be enough to cover the taxes for Jesus and his disciples.

Matthew 17:27 *"Notwithstanding, lest we should offend them, go thou to the sea, and cast an hook, and take up the fish that first cometh up; and when thou hast opened his mouth, thou shalt find a piece of money: that take, and give unto them for me and thee."*

Allow me to tell you of one more financial miracle demonstrated to us by Jesus, our example. Jesus saw two ships standing by the lake. The fishermen were gone out of them, and they were washing their nets. Jesus entered into Simon's ship and asked him to thrust out a little from the land. He taught the people out of the ship. Then he told Peter to "Launch out into the deep, and let down your nets for a draught (haul of fish)." Peter was reluctant because they had taken nothing all night. But he finally conceded and said, "Nevertheless at thy word I will let down the net." Notice what the Bible says happened next,

Luke 5:6 *"And when they had this done, they enclosed a great multitude of fishes: and their net brake."*

This was such a tremendous multitude of fishes that their net broke. They beckoned unto their partners in the other ship that they should come and help them. Both ships were filled and began to sink. This represents financial overflow. These fishermen knew this was a miracle. I hope you know it as well. They were astonished by it. James and John who were partners with Simon Peter knew they could take the multitude of fishes and sell them. They could make a tremendous profit.

III John verse 2 *"Beloved, I wish above all things that thou mayest prosper and be in health, even as thy soul prospereth."*

Satan who opposed their vision and purpose of catching fish had been defeated by Jesus our Savior. I think we should believe the song Tamela Mann sings called, "God Will Provide." He will give financial miracles to those who believe him. God can cause you and I to get things at a very amazing low price, or he can raise our finances up to an amazing high level to buy the item that seemed out of our price range. Either way God gets the glory for delivering people from the financial oppression that Satan thought to be their demise.

I encourage you to believe God to make financial miracles a part of your life. The world system controlled by the god of this world seeks to keep people bogged down in a financial rut or shortage. It causes them to live with anxiety and stress. Jesus admonished us to take no thought about what we are going to eat, drink, or wear. He told us that our Heavenly Father knows that we need these things.

The enemy wants our attention to be on the natural things instead of spiritual things. He wants our minds off God. God wants our hearts and mind on him. God will give you financial miracles so you can keep the attention on him. It is hard to stay focused on God when you are concerned about being put out of your house or having your lights turned off. This is why those of us who have been empowered financially seek to help our brothers and sisters in Christ who have a need in these areas.

I John 3:16,17 *"But whoso hath this world's good, and seeth his brother have need, and shutteth up his bowels of compassion from him, how dwelleth the love of God in him?"*

Sometimes a financial miracle comes in the form of you getting a good job. God is able to give you a job that is above your educational level or something that you don't have a degree in. He will cause his favor to open up the heart of those who are in authority and hire you for the position. He will then cause bonuses and raises to be given to you beyond anything you can dream or imagine.

Proverbs 21:1 *"The king's heart is in the hand of the Lord, as the rivers of water: he turneth it whithersoever he will."*

ENEMIES BEWARE GOD IS STILL AT WORK!

(MIRACLE TESTIMONIES)

Years ago my lovely sister-in-law, Marjorie Sharpe gave me a word from God. She told me that God said, "Be encourage. Enemies beware God is at work." This might not seem like much to you, but at that time that prophetic word edified, exhorted and comforted me. It propelled my life to do many of the dynamic things that I've been able to do and achieve today. Thank you Marjorie!

John 5:17 *"But Jesus answered them, My Father worketh hitherto, and I work."*

This verse shows us one of the many reasons why we should expect miracles to still be a part of our lives today. God hasn't stopped healing through us. He hasn't stopped honoring the faith of those who choose to believe. The same God that still forgives sins, still heals and works miracles.

Psalms 103:3 (Mofatts Translation)
"He pardons all your sins, and all your sicknesses he heals."

I will seek to list some modern day miracles relating to the healing of the body and the financial arena that I hope and pray will give you the faith for your miracle or the miracle of your loved one. Please know that we aren't saying you will never die, but I believe if we are going to live out the fullness of our days and maximize our potential, then we must see miracles. These are real people with real testimonies. Their names are not fake or phony. They along with their family members have decided to share their testimonies with you.

Psalms 105:1 *"O give thanks unto the LORD; call upon his name: make known his deeds among the people."*

PERSONAL TESTIMONIES

1. MY OWN TESTIMONY—Van Sharpe. In 1982, I was applying for a job with the Edgecombe County School System. It required that I get a physical. During the physical I was diagnosed with a sign of tuberculosis. I was a single young man staying with my mother. I came home and went into the living room (my prayer room at that time). I reminded God that my body belonged to him, and I believed him to heal my body. When I went back to the doctor a few days later, I was totally healed. Hallelujah!

2. MY WIFE'S TESTIMONY—Resunester Sharpe. In 1983, my wife had a cyst on her back near her buttocks. It was so painful that she could barely walk. She had to walk bowed together, and we were scheduled to be married at the beginning of 1984 in February to be exact. She was living in Reidsville with her mom. I went to her home to pick her up to come to the local church that I had just started to pastor. When I arrived, she was upstairs and bowed together. I began to pray in the Holy

Spirit. The Lord spoke to me plainly and said, "Take her back with you to Tarboro. On the way back I will heal her." I told her and her mom what the Lord spoke to me. Her mom smiled and said, "Aww, you just want to get her down there in Tarboro to that church." I explained to her that she was incorrect that the Lord had really spoken this to me. My wife got her things, and she drove back to Tarboro in my mother's (Shirley Sharpe) car. I fell asleep on the way back because I had been preaching and teaching a lot that week. It was on a Friday evening and as we arrived on the other side of Durham my wife yelled out. I awakened and asked her what had happened. She said, "I think something has happen to the cyst." She pulled the car over to the side of the road. She got up out of the seat and we noticed blood and pus was all over the seat. The cyst had burst and blood and pus had come through her dress onto the seat of the front seat of my mother's car where she was sitting. We both began to give God praise because we knew that our God had kept his word. He had healed her on the way back to Tarboro just like he had spoken. I was so excited. I could hardly wait until I got back home to my mother's house and call my wife's mom. As soon as I arrived home, I gave her mom a call and told her the good news. She seemed happy. However, after the weekend was over. She took Resunester to the doctor to get it checked out. Her mom was a little skeptical since she wasn't saved at that time. The doctor checked the area out and said, "Ms. Sophronia I thought I would need to lance the area to get the pus and blood out, but when I looked at the area, someone has already lanced it." Halleijuah! God lanced it without leaving a mark or a scar. Ain't God good! Yes, he still works miracles.

3. MY WIFE AGAIN—Resunester Sharpe. In 1997, my wife had a cyst on her hand. I took her to the doctor, and he drew out the fluid inside of the cyst with a needle. My wife plays the keyboard and due to the fact that her hands are constantly being worked in this fashion, the doctor told her that even though he drew it out this time, it would eventually come back. Well one day I was preaching on television

about healing on a local station in Rocky Mount called WHIG-TV. It was live and my wife was at home watching the live progam. After I preached the word, I told those who were sick to touch that part of their bodies as I prayed for the sick. She laid hands on her hand. The cyst disappeared immediately, and it hasn't returned since back since. Hallelujah!

4. MY DAUGHTER'S TESTIMONY-- Vanneika Sharpe. In 1991, my daughter was born and at her birth there was a major concern. The nurse couldn't find a heartbeat while she was inside my wife's womb. My wife and I prayed and when the doctor came in to examine my wife, he (the doctor) found all to be well. Hallelujah! Also, when she was five years old, she was taken to the hospital because she was having some chest pains. It was there that the doctors told us that she had asthma. They wanted to fly her in a helicopter to Greenville immediately. My wife and I both knew that Vanneika was a blessed child because she was ours, and we began to laugh after the doctor left the room. I heard the Lord speak to me as plain as day. He told me

to leave the hospital and take Vanneika home. He told me that she would be fine. My wife and I left the hospital and didn't return until the next time for her to get a physical. Today she is in her late twenties. She has graduated from A&T State University with a degree in Graphic Design and employed at a company in Greensboro. God is good!

5. MY GRANDSON'S TESTIMONY—Taiden Sharpe. In 2011, my daughter was pregnant with my first grandchild. She was told that if she kept this child that he would be a Down syndrome child. She had one of two alternatives. She could have an abortion, or she could give birth to a Down syndrome child and seek to raise him the best way she could. I remember my daughter coming downstairs with tears in her eyes. As a father, I assured her that aborting the child wasn't an option, but we were going to believe God for a healthy child. I reminded her of the many testimonies that she had seen God work in the lives of others, and God wasn't going to let her down, especially since she was seeking to do the right thing. Well today

Taiden is six years old and counting. He is a special young boy who when he was 2 years old loved to sing the song "Our God is Awesome" by Charles Jenkins. He is a vibrant young boy. Praise the Lord!

6. MY BROTHER'S TESTIMONY—Wayne Sharpe. In 1991, my brother was diagnosed with meningitis. Meningitis is a rare infection that inflames the delicate membranes—called the meninges—that cover the brain and spinal cord. It causes severe headaches and stiffness in the neck. Bacterial meningitis can be life-threatening and spreads between people in close contact with each other. Wayne was in the hospital in Raleigh, N.C. and my sister, mom and I along with his wife, Marjorie knew that we needed to surround him with prayer. On my way to Raleigh, I knew it was important to be in faith. I listened to healing tapes all the way from Rocky Mount to Raleigh.

When we arrived at the hospital, we were told to wear masks and gloves before we entered the room. As we walked in, the doctor was talking to his wife concerning my brother's condition. I knew he was trying to tell her as best he could that my brother wasn't going to live. Finally, I interrupted him and said, "Ok doctor. What you are trying to say is that my brother isn't going to make it. He is going to die right?" The doctor responded with a "yes," and he left the room. I was thinking in my mind that it was good the doctor left because we could get down to prayer.

As we began to surround his bed and pray, we began to speak in other tongues. The Holy Ghost spoke through me that he would live and not die, and declare the works of the Lord. He told me that the glory of the latter house would be greater than the former house. My sister began to prophecy over him that the Lord was going to raise him up and that he would do even a greater work for the Lord than he had done thus far.

Today he is a Bishop, and his local church is growing. They have paid off a several hundred thousand dollar facility. They have purchased six acres on Capital Boulevard in Raleigh. He is in the process of building a brand new home and a brand new sanctuary. Hallelujah! He has no brain damage or lack of memory.

You might think he is lucky. No, he is a testimony of the miracle working power of God Almighty. Later we found out that in the hospital room on his left and the hospital room on his right, the patients who had the same disease (meningitis) died. My brother Bishop Wayne Sharpe is alive preaching and teaching like a man from another world because God still works miracles!

7. SAINT'S TESTIMONY—Joyce Ann (Brown) Archer. In 1976 at the tender age of 15 years old she was diagnosed with cancer. She had been in and out of Chapel Hill Hospital for many years. Her family had to constantly travel from Tarboro to Chapel Hill or spend many nights staying there. Finally, the doctors had done all they could do to try to save her life. They eventually sent her home to die. My sister and I along with her praying mother, Mary Brown, prayed for her anointing her with oil. She went back to the doctors and no cancer was found in her body. She not only lived but she had two boys when the doctors thought she could never have children. God is amazing! She lived to be 41. It is

important to note that devil didn't take her out with cancer. I have the healing report in my office drawer, and I keep it as a constant reminder that the name of Jesus is bigger than cancer.

8. SAINT'S TESTIMONY—Elizabeth A. Harrell. In 1989, she was diagnosed with breast cancer. She found a knot in her right breast and a biopsy taken by her doctor came back positive for breast cancer. She had to believe God for her healing. Through and by the hearing of faith, she has been healed now for almost 28 years and counting. Hallelujah! It has never returned. To God be all the glory!

9. SAINT'S TESTIMONY—Eugenia Draughn. In 2010, she had a stroke, and she had a brain aneurism in 2014. Due to the severity of these things, she should be paralyzed, have memory loss, have some kind of speech impediment, or she could even be dead. I remember when she was in the hospital in Greenville as God was restoring her body back to wholeness, she would walk the halls singing the song "Incredible God Incredible Praise" by Youthful Praise featuring James Hairston. It became her victory song as well as her

testimony concerning the God that she serves. She truly believes in praising him. All that her body went through affected the right side of her body. She had to learn how to walk all over again, but today she walks unassisted without any cane or walker. Give God Praise!

10. SAINT'S TESTIMONY—EVANGELINE WHITAKER. In 2011, she had to have an operation on her head to remove a benign tumor that was trapped between her brain and skull. The church made intercession for her on a continual basis before the operation was scheduled to take place. We were in faith along with her husband (Edward), her daughter (Rachel), and the rest of her family. I remember telling her daughter that we don't know what God is going to do, but we know he will do something. I said to her that when the doctors go in and look, they might not even find anything. Well God didn't do that, but he still gave her a miracle that amazed even the doctors. The doctors made a small incision on the top of the benign tumor. It immediately popped out, "Poop." It was the size of a golf ball. Today she has no dizziness or

loss of proper balance. She is alive and well and giving God praise every single day. Thank you Jesus!

11. SAINT'S TESTIMONY—Mary Alice Brown. In 2003, she was called to the doctor's office to be given an update on some test that she had taken because she had a cough that she just couldn't get rid of. She asked my wife and I if we could go with her to talk with the doctor. We said, "Yes, no problem." We arrived at the hospital, and the doctor came in and told us the results of the tests. The doctor told us that they had found a tumor about the size of a grapefruit in her body. They suggested that she allow them to fly her to the Greenville hospital or that we drive her there immediately. He said that they would probably have to cut her from one side of her body to the other to remove this type of aggressive looking tumor. He told her that the longer she waited the larger it would probably get until it would eventually lead to her death. I remember when we walked out of that hospital with Mary Brown, a mother in our church, that there was so much I wanted to say to

try to comfort her. But I said nothing and neither did my wife. Finally, when we got to the hospital parking lot, Mother Brown said to me, "Pastor I don't want to be cut on." She said, "My body is the temple of the Holy Ghost, and I believe God to heal my body." I wanted to jump in the air at that very moment because her words were my exact sentiments. I said to her that I was glad to hear that because we know God is able to heal especially since the Lord had called our local church family on a shut-in, which consisted of fasting and praying. Mother Brown shared with my wife and I that she didn't want everyone to know about what the doctors had found She didn't even want her immediate family to know because she said that they might be all upset and talk doubt to her. The shut-in started on Friday afternoon at 6 p.m. We prayed and read our Bibles all through the night. It is a time of intense praying and making supplication to the Lord. It was during that time that my wife whispered to me that it was time to lay hands on Mother Brown for her healing. I took out the anointing oil and called her up to the front of the church. I laid hands on her and commanded the cancer to die and leave her body in the name of Jesus. She fell out under the heavy presence of the Lord. A few days later she went back to the doctor, and he could find no trace of cancer in her body. Even to this very day every year when she gets her examination, she is cancer free. Hallelujah! We are still shouting the victory and giving God all the glory. The name of Jesus is still making a difference. God still heals!

12. SAINT'S TESTIMONY—Iris White. In August, 2014 she was having back problems and went in to get checked out. Little did she know that during what looked like a simple routine check-up would turn into something as horrific as finding out that she had Renal Cell Carcinoma (kidney cancer). She was told that the tumors would take over her kidneys and shut them down and the cancer would eventually take over her whole body. She was told a kidney operation was necessary because they were 99.9 % positive that it was kidney cancer. The operation was needed

in order to remove her entire kidney because she could still live with one kidney. When she called my wife and I on the phone and told us about it, we recommended that she meet us at the church immediately. We met with her and her daughter (Shontae) at the church. In my office my wife made a copy for her whole family of a healing outline from teachings that I have done over the years concerning healing. I read them through with her and her daughter and admonished her to take copies home for her husband (Marvin) and her son (Marvin Jr.). I told her not to let anyone speak doubt around her. Then my wife and I walked with her into the sanctuary and laid hands on her anointing her with oil. I command the cancer to die and leave her body in Jesus' name. I said, "Be healed from the crown of your head to the soles of your feet." She fell out under the powerful presence of God. When she arose to her feet, I told her to remember this day for this was the day that she got her healing. It was September 11, 2014. I told her no matter what the doctors said or anybody else said this was the day of her deliverance. She smiled and agreed. I could tell she was ready for this faith fight. She had lost two sisters due to cancer, but she wasn't about to be the third one. Her husband was strong in faith and so was she. We told her to listen to healing Cd's and watch Gloria Copeland, Sandra Kennedy, Kenneth Hagin, Fred Price, Creflo Dollar, and others who taught about healing on You Tube. Every time we would see anyone teaching or giving healing testimonies on television my wife would call her to make sure that she watched them. This was a fight we were determined to help her win. She was always willing to watch it. The devil had picked on the wrong one this time. On the day that her operation was scheduled, my wife and I were just getting back in town from another state. We arrived at the hospital just in time to pray with her and the family along with my brother (Bishop Wayne Sharpe) and his wife (Marjorie). When they took her back into the operating room to supposedly have her kidney removed, God had worked the miracle that even they (the doctors) could not deny. Yes, a notable miracle had taken place. They couldn't find any trace of cancer in her body. Hallelujah! Hallelujah! She still has both of her kidneys in place and gives God all the praise for making her whole.

13. SAINT'S TESTIMONY--Kiante Deshon Hines. In June 2016, he came to our local church in a wheel chair at age twenty five. He had been diagnosed with multiple sclerosis when he was sixteen. At age eighteen, the disease caused him to have to be put in a wheel chair. The doctors had said that he would never walk again due to the disease that caused his muscles to deteriorate. He was also diagnosed with polyneuropathy, which is a disease affecting peripheral nerves in roughly the same areas of the on both sides of the body. It causes weakness, numbness, and burning pain. The Sunday that his family members brought him to the church, I preached a message entitled "Favored and Empowered to Exercise Your Spiritual Authority." While I was preaching, I could see that he was mixing faith with the word of God coming out of my mouth. After I finished, I asked those who wanted to be prayed for to

come to the altar. His family brought him up to the front first. The devil began to talk. I could hear him say, "Aren't you going look stupid when you pray for this young man and he doesn't get healed?" I shut him out with the word as I thought about the man lying at the gate called beautiful. I was going to believe God for this miracle. I laid my hands on him anointing him with oil in Jesus' name. I commanded him to be healed from the crown of his head to the soles of his feet. Then I told him to arise and walk. He got out of the wheel chair and walked liked someone who has been walking for years. Hallelujah! Hallelujah! He pushed the wheel chair in the sanctuary. We started praising God in the house of the Lord. We knew God had confirmed his word with signs following. Indeed a notable miracle had taken place. It was one that nobody present could deny. The name of Jesus had been exalted and sickness and disease had been defeated once again. I told Keonte since he had gotten healed that he needed to assist me in praying for the sick. He stood up the rest of the service and did just that.

Glory to God in the Highest! He has bee.
walking from that day to this one. Thank
you Lord!

14. SAINT'S TESTIMONY—Doris Hodges.
In April 2017, she was experiencing a
pain that she was unable to get rid of.
She was told by a doctor that she had
a stomach virus, and her doctor put
her on some antibiotics. However, her
pain continued, and she went to the
hospital because she felt that her heart
wasn't beating properly. The hospital
sent her home and told her within a
few days that they wanted her to take a
stress test. However, her two daughters
(Beatrice and Mary Ann) recommended
that she get a second opinion. On
that Saturday night the Lord spoke to
Mother Doris. She heard the Lord say,
"Greenville, Greenville." She called my
wife and I and told us that she was still
in pain and wanted to go get another
opinion. She told us what she heard the
Lord say, and we told her to go do it.
She called her daughter (Beatrice) and
her son (Anthony) to take her to the
Greenville Hospital. Once she arrived,
they discovered that her appendix had

burst, and they also found two cysts on her gall bladder. The reason I am telling this story is because it truly shows that it pays to listen to the Holy Ghost. He told her where to go in order to get her miracle or else she would have died being treated for the wrong thing. Hallelujah! Instead of a funeral for one of the mothers in our church, we had had a praise party! Thank You God!

There are many more powerful testimonies that I could share with you, but I just wanted to give you enough to stir your awareness of God's power and also encourage you to share your healing or financial testimony with others. The need to do so is crucial to help raise the level of faith and expectation among people in our country and abroad. God is at work, and he needs us to tell of his goodness. If you and I fail to do so, we cause a generation to suffer needlessly because they don't know that there is a way of escape through the power of Miracles!

Psalm 145:4-7 *"One generation shall praise thy works to another, and shall declare thy mighty acts. [5] I will speak of the glorious*

*honour of thy majesty; and of thy wondrous
works. [6] And men shall speak of the might
of thy terrible acts: and I will declare thy
greatness. [7] They shall abundantly utter
the memory of thy great goodness, and shall
sing of thy righteousness."*

Your testimony is your way of investing into the next generation. You shouldn't go to the grave without passing your story of God's power on to your children and grandchildren. They need to know where God brought you from. They need to know how God blessed you. I have seen people in the church that I pastor who were given cars, given houses, given major home appliances, given money, and given land God has been truly amazing! These types of things position people to look to God to show them his ability to provide. Remember when you share your testimony you are investing your life into someone else's.

Jim Rohn said, "Investing Life into Life has the potential of creating miracles."

CONCLUSION

Judges 6:13 *"And Gideon said unto him, Oh my Lord, if the LORD be with us, why then is all this befallen us? and where be all his miracles which our fathers told us of, saying, Did not the LORD bring us up from Egypt? but now the LORD hath forsaken us, and delivered us into the hands of the Midianites."*

In my conclusion, I remind you to put your faith back in God. We will fall apart or lose our minds without believing in miracles. The adversary knows that he is running out of time. Jesus' return is imminent. Satan has put out an all points bulletin against humanity. He is throwing everything he can at you and I to hinder the work of God. We must not allow him to use who died or who suffered a tragedy to cause doubt to fester its ugly head.

God does his greatest work in the midst of trouble. We must tell everyone we meet that God works masterfully in dark times. Many will try everything else before they finally see the need to rely upon God Almighty.

Some of you need to recognize that your very life has been a miracle. There is no way you would be where you are or have what you have without God's intervention. He has interrupted Satan's plan and purpose to destroy you and I over and over again. God blocked the enemy's plan with a miracle. It is exciting to know that the answer to the question asked by Gideon can be answered. Miracles are still available, and they are still happening!

G. K. Chesterton "The most incredible thing about miracles is that they happen."